COMMON GROUND

COMMON GROUND

D A PRINCE

Happen*Stance*

By the same author:

Nearly the Happy Hour, Happen*Stance,* 2008
Undoing Time, Pikestaff, 1998
Without Boundaries, Manifold, 2001
Keeping in Touch, Pikestaff, 2002

First published in 2014 by Happen*Stance*
21 Hatton Green, Glenrothes, Fife KY7 4SD
www.happenstancepress.com

Printed and bound in the UK by
Berforts Information Press, Stevenage

ISBN 978-1-910131-03-9

CONTENTS

COMMON GROUND

For David

Everything I know about

hanging wallpaper came from a West End play,
early 70s, title and playwright lost,
even the plot. But two actors he-ing and she-ing—
unrolling, measuring, cutting, pasting, folding,
unpleating each length every night of the run—
they taught me.

My sister sent knitting instructions, second class,
dense blue biro on a postcard I kept for years.
Fountains Abbey in autumn light:
the neatest way to join shoulder seams.

Laying bricks, from a novel by Solzhenitsyn
(though I've never put that into practice)
unlike sex, from so many novels
the library shelves are exhausted.

There was the man in the laundrette
who could fold a perfect fitted sheet
and everything I know about the Ramones
I learned from a poem.

The good poems

look up, eye the sky, and whistle
a half-caught air, part
sucked away on the breeze
swinging the weather vane all ways.

They lean forward just enough.
They leave a scrap of space around the shadow
which might be a cat or flagpole or grandmother
or none of the above.

You can't tell where they start.
That first line with its sense of direction
is just to fool you. It all began
long before this, and ends

long after this book is closed,
somewhere else, and sometimes
in another country. Don't worry:
they still enjoy your company.

Dance Class

It was *heel toe one two three turn*
and shuffling to arithmetic and arguing
about who would lead this time, until
the student came and recognised
our concentration on the waltz's triangle,
the mutterings, our plimsolls lined up to escape
Miss Taylor's *no no no*.
Not to be trusted with the heavy weights
of grammar, or imponderables
like filling leaking baths or trains
racing at variable speeds,
she eyed our leaden feet, and promised:
trees.

So half a term the loud winds dance us, shake
and bend and whip and whirl and storm and sway
our green limbs through their seasons.
Barefoot, with cardigans reversed on branching arms,
their buttons wriggling up our spines,
we let our twiggy fingers ripple
into leaves. We understand
the pulse and rhythm of a living wood, our toes
alive and tuned in to the earth. Just half a term

and in stamped the Gay Gordons. Mothers bought
new plimsolls, complaining
how we'd grown, but pleased
with our Veletas, our stiff Skaters' Waltz.

Gulliver

In a grimy town with no bookshops, *Gulliver*
comes lording it out of Woolworths
in Regency Classics crimson, shiny
with status under a scuffed jacket.

Trampling over *The Three Musketeers*,
The Last of the Mohicans—titles
off Sunday teatime telly and tinned fruit—
he lilliputs us into place.

In the grained creak of yellow pages
he's the big man who's travelled, seen life,
spine snapping to attention, keeping his head
among the tiny fidgets brushing his feet.

So far above and away from us,
two and sixpenny immortal, he could be God.
Under the bedclothes, read in a crack of light,
he's every solution, drawing a fleet of answers.

Even when he's grounded, threads tight
with the muscle of him, I can't believe he'd fall.

What's My Line?

Black and white Sunday evenings, the week ahead
laid out in its grid, and the day of rest
packed away with the best table cloth.
The creamy voice of Eamonn Andrews
settles us down, at ease with the exotic
of black bow ties, and Lady Isobel
in strapless glitter. They live,
we think, like this, amused by mime,
raising their eyebrows, teasing out
our weekday selves, the labels sewn
into our socks. Their rest of the week sits
on the shoulders of the likes of us.

Horatio

Always in shadow, on the edge, the light
falling on someone else. I'm used to it—
fidus Achates, and half-acolyte.
Besides, the sidelines are a safer bet
so I survive—at least, upon the page,
though never in imagination.
The curtain falls: I vanish with the stage.
Even Rosencrantz and Guildenstern live on
in other times, but I—the dutiful
and sober pal, the philosophic friend—
dissolve. I fade. Meanwhile, the beautiful
capture your soul beyond the play's neat end
where I'm to set, with due fidelity,
the record straight. You won't remember me.

Looking at *Hamlet*

Parents don't help. And who d'you ask
about dead fathers, mothers quick to snatch
a murderer for a bedmate?

Besides, we're closer to Ophelia, arguing
what happens in the darkness, in the wings,
what edge she struggled on, how long,
where the first hairline crack appeared.
Did she say *it doesn't matter*, brush
an eyelash from her cheek? In some lights
was it invisible, smoothed over?
We sieve her words in huddles out of class,
awed by what love has done offstage.
No clues to choice or chance. Poor puppet—
only riddles, flowers, and the graveyard scene.

Advanced Level

What sort of knife? He's driven dumper trucks
on building sites, he says (his student days)
and thinks it a fair question. This 'Isabel,
poor simple Isabel!'—not like she's one of us.
He eyes the room, sharp to the reflex twitch
a hand might make checking its blade.
Nobody's moved and, ready to relax,
he creaks his chair on two back legs, stretching.
He's pulled the poem up to date, made Keats
suddenly streetwise. And so we pause,
the subject hanging, tangled
in our collective ignorance: of Florence
and Boccaccio, a woman's place,
the whole Renaissance world.
He glints. *Where'd she get this knife?*

*Her brothers stank with money so
she's not the type for kitchen work.*
Licking the question's hollow edge
he's after blood. *A penknife, then?* envisaging
exquisite inlay, scrolls of foliage,
the delicacy of boudoir lace;
a lady's hand, precise in what it does.
And when she's dug with it (stroking his neck
reflectively), *exposing the decay, she . . .*
Stops.
How long. . . ? And stops again.

So this is love, the unconditional love
that after death has gouged through skin, hair, flesh,
the sinews, veins, down to the bone; has clawed
and scratched, hour after hour, until
it has its trophy. Love. The winner.
Love that can't let go, that conjures all its ghosts
as souvenirs. Love

beyond the *True Life Stories*, magazines
stacking up happy promises like dirty bombs.
Love that in June explodes into exams—
Discuss with reference to the text . . .

He shifts. *Forget the knife.* How can we? It's the point
we cling to, after. *Would-you. . . ? Could-you. . . ?*
Poor Isabel, how we've advanced
in half an afternoon but only just begun
the lifelong slide. *Love*: that word
scored as graffiti, driven into dreams
or nightmares, now too late
to pack away like school books. *And next week—*
he says—*we're moving on to later works.*

Memo to Self

If I want to make you suffer, I put in
where, wiper, window—the *www*—
your mouth gags on.
And *aaa*—gets you running for cover,
from *aardvark* to *arquebus*.

I hold your tongue to them, get you
forcing your lips round their wobble, the way
they stick like wallpaper to your teeth,
their waywardness. Wicked!

A whole script of misery: *Why
is the warbler whistling? Is Walthamstow wet?*
I could go on; I could force-feed you
with memory till you're speechless,
leave you choked.

But enough. Let's just say this:
while you're grown-up now, and smarter
than a stumbling school-kid, you're no wiser.
There's always that witch weaving spells,
waiting to whisk you way back.
It's only for today we've got it licked.

This Morning

What do you say over toughened toast
and coffee flaked with the milk's sour rim
and the radio competing for attention?

That the crumbs crunched into the floor
still sound like sand? That it might rain?

You can talk round the edge, avoiding
how the morning is bleached beyond comparing
after night shone its searchlight into your dream.

That glare of love, the realignment
of daylight's geometry,
is reconsidering you. In the tick of the clock

you stare into marmalade, wondering
where to begin and how much this wakening
has torn you adrift from yesterday's harbour.

Next Morning

When at last we speak you deliver
the facts of Condorcet, briefly:
why the Paris statue we both know carries a book
and how, biographically,
the Stanhope connection came about.

Then I comment on the rain. Not the dream
loosening the night, how we were living
in irregular rooms, the floors
uncarpeted and holes to the cellars,
and no food for our friends
who were polite but puzzled.

No songbirds sing.
Outside, only a quarrel
between a magpie and a squirrel.

How to run for this clock

Someone has unlocked language,
packing it in a new pattern
he thinks we understand.

Adjust time from the back side button
with hands on the exact position.
Ah, yes; the perfect timing.

When I put *batteries in container for clock running,*
the second hand mouths its silent tick.
It clicks around the minutes, translating
its numbers into bus timetables, cooking spaghetti,
sunset as printed in the diary;
starting to run me.

In dark night I can *glow the dial*
for full time watching. Sharing this
will see us through to morning, when
I must *avoid to beam the sun directly.*

So many warnings. And I am assured
that if no one turns off the switch
it will *continuously alarm me.*

All the Time in the World

And while we're away
the silenced locks sit tight, holding back
the company of clocks ticking
to an audience of empty rooms.
No one hears the gruff cough
when the hour's almost due, before
the pulling-together of weights and cogs
gearing up for the chime.

The hours are measuring themselves.

They don't need us to tell them
how to fill the unforgiving minute,
to lecture them on history, to slice
them, trim them, take their ragged edges off.
They *are*. Just that. There's something enviable
in their completeness, their austere reserve,
diminishing us. They've spent their time
in contemplating stillness, like clean space
between the seconds. Now we're home
they feign indifference, whisper to the clocks
to spread their hands, cover their faces, track
the circles till it's time for us to leave.

The New Machine

Unskinned it smells of fish
(the oiling, father says). Metals
glint that same watered silver, slip
and slough their bubble wrap,
return the light's glance.

They gather round. *Don't touch.*
The child takes back her hand
fingering the moment, all she's overheard,
what it can do, will save,
might lead to. The angel in the barn
gleams back, triumphant.

Ridding

In hard weather the old words come back,
the ones we used to laugh at, mocking
their lack of travel. *Fair clemmed*,
when mean winds scoured the gutters,
better to *bide*, stay *thrutched in*
like hens in a coop. This was getting by,
nothing to *scrat* for, and now the words fit
rightly. We're still growing into them
faster each winter, when we're *mithered*;
back to their *mardy* childhood sound.

So much, now. Who will do the *ridding*
when the snow piles up, hiding the trodden paths,
the tracks that got us here? Then
the *ridding* after that.

The Old Words

Dawnbreak they come to me, heads in their hands,
parodies of ghosts. They have planned this,
been planning this, the old words.

Heal us whole, their mouths whisper.
Deal us discoveries, inventions, the untrodden.
Give us galaxies for wandering.

How long have they haunted here
where even the echoes are silenced?

What are they finding for the future, for
the trespass of travel, their faces
unfreezing in the new weather?

Make us mandrakes.
Clep us chemistries.

Plead us the Pleiades.

Perseids

We planned to catch one, each of us,
and slipped out late into the thickening dark
with Eddie's brother's keep-net and a sack.

We guessed the lake would fill its shallows
tracking the dot-dash stars sizzling above, even
the moon's pimply silence lurking behind the ash.

Pride of place for the Nature Table, and Miss
being chuffed; better than galls or stitchwort; more
than the lumpy pellet Philip claimed was *owl*.

Too early for green apples. There were clouds
and Tom went home. *Hungry*, he said. And so
were we, but clutched it close, to stay.

Ducks kicked up a rumpus, scuffed the water
into reedy scum. Kevin swore. This was no way
to plot the falling of a star and, out of our depth,

we knew the project shot. They'd be out for us now,
back home, the leather ready. *What time
d'you call this?* But the shower, when it came—

like light whistling and calling overhead, playing
tag in relays, hurdling—grabbed all our gasps,
left us gawping in the wake of fizzled air:

empty-handed, nothing to show,
everything to chase after.

London Streets

Every so often weather barges in,
shakes their shoulders, tells them *Look!*
this is how it is.

The traffic stops, sticks in the gutters,
sulks into listening like children who
took too much for granted. *How many times. . . ?*

Too late for a second chance when winter
clenches a fist, flattens a flag-staff or two,
unfaces the hands on the clock.

Weather spreads its arms—not
a loving hug or the mateyness of meeting up
but menace: *THIS big*

vodka glistening on its breath.

Fen Celery

Two-pairs-of-socks-and-mittens weather.
Out on the fen an easterly sifts soil,
driving its soot deep down tomorrow's stems.
The pale ribs gleam. As raw as winter hands
the day's cold harvest earths the market stall
to country roots, the tough wind's slap of salt,
smell of December under snag-toothed frost,
the crunch of trodden ice in gutters.

Back-kitchen work. The chop and scrape and scrub,
over and over, water running black
and ancient. No short cuts. The real stuff.
Your grimy nails explore each ridge and strip
down to the heart, still searching out
this clean-sweat smell under the silt, the source.

Soup

At the end of the month it's often swede but even this
with garlic, a small onion, perhaps a stick
of celery, maybe that carrot dried out in the fridge—
you could do worse. The garlic comes
from taking childhood taste,
growing it up, and learning.
A fresh-pulled bay leaf helps (and if there's time
ruffle the dead leaves underneath: breathe in).
The parsley on the windowsill, all stalk,
gives off its winter-watery smell.
The pepper cosies up.
                              Or when it's leeks
down to half-price, and potatoes left
from weekend baking, or sweet parsnips, there's
a thicker warmth to insulate the house
against hard times, rooted in winter, lasting
longer than you think.

New Year

After the glitter, tinsel, baubles
in gilt and silver, after the sheen
of wrapping paper, sparkling string,
the restless on-off Christmas lights,
the tinkling carols from a radio;
after stretched smiles aching for bedtime,
the tired company and sausage rolls
and kisses, the fired-up heating,
glazed condensation, the shrivelling holly

there comes to the emptied table

a spray of winter jasmine clean as spring
with its young yellow, and a blue bowl
of russet apples flushed with Indian summer
and a longer light.

A Real Cat Poem

Kittens?—the vet had seen to that
at just six months. Her fur grew back,
softer at first; the knotted thread dissolved.
You'd never know.

Sex?—that's a different story.
Queues formed each morning, feral bruisers
eyeing her, jostling, suddenly silent.
She stared them out.

And then? I'd work to get to,
schedules and such. She wore a patient look,
resigned. She never showed the scars.
I didn't ask.

Abigail

A name for next door's new baby, she says,
but it opens a crack back
to when Abigail from Accounts, who'd spent
every weekend for years plastering,
papering, painting with her intended
so marriage would be show-house splendid
suddenly gave back her diamond, and swapped him
for his best friend.
                    And among the Tippex, carbons,
golf-ball typewriters firing out letters, spider plants,
shorthand, the cakes-on-birthdays routines,
we were greasy with curiosity:
how it didn't add up, what words he'd spluttered,
whether they'd thrown anything, and wondering
what would happen now to all that wallpaper.

It couldn't happen

but suppose the door-bell rang—
you, greasy jeans, and thinking Trick or treat?
another pizza flyer?—and there's
a uniform, the whole street blocked,
the gold-glass glitter of a coach
and four matched bays, shrinking Ted's van
and Gupta's 4x4, curtains
already twitching *Who d'she think she is?*
waving gloved hands (oh, pigeon-breast,
those gloves!):
                 Madam, the Prince awaits
                 your presence at the Ball.
                 Your fairy godmother has sent her coach.
the first impatience of a car
snarling its horn, the 88
(already late) giving the upstairs deck
a papparazzi view, a row of phones
fast-track to YouTube—

what would you do?

There you go!

Here you are with your life dangling
plastic over a '2 for £5' tee-shirt,
ID flashing a chubby photo grinning
when your hair was darker and
there wasn't only fifteen minutes left on your break,
checkout fumbling each bar code,
everyone paying by card, system
struggling, the month too long for the money,
the tannoy begging Mr Jones to come to the phone,
somebody's split pack leaking sugar,
forgetting to bring a bag again,
settling for the own brands, the Value,
the Everyday, what they'll eat without fussing,
and the same lopsided sign-off.

Here you are telling Lisa, later, lighting up
by bins over-bulged with black plastic,
freed from your screens, spinning out Marlboroughs,
laughing where you'd like to be, given the chance
or Lottery, always the same unlucky numbers,
photos winking at each other, when she cuts in
Nah and *They don't call it tannoy no more*,
so that's one more fuck-up, owed
to your mam's scrapbook phrases, the ones you'd scoffed at—
return half of a ticket, shillings for the gas,
how the doctor knows best, suffer in silence,
take a Rainmate just in case,
when it was *Mind how you go!* and a peck,
always making the best of a bad job.

Heading Back

Here you are: bus queue, Co-op carrier
creasing your hands, Mr Tattoo in front
gleaming with all-day sweat, outside *Cash Advances Loans*
Cheques Cashed (No Questions), next to
Lucky-7 Amusements, down from
PriceBuster (bills and pizza flyers piling up
behind bankrupt glass) across the street
Paddy Power Bookmakers and two 'To Let';

frozen prawns leaking sea-smell on a sliced loaf,
cut-price tomatoes squashing to pulp,
your pass stuck under the bills you meant to pay
but didn't, *Pensioner mugged for 50p*
as the evening headline. Hoping for a seat,
not much to ask, not too much.

Until they close

they sell the nails, screws, nameless clips and clamps
(*DIY Sundries* claims their peeling sign)
for one-off needs discovered when the house
won't hold together. Glues, like nowhere else.
Fillers for making good. Odd lengths of wood.
Lists you'd never thought of on an average day.
Papers for rubbing down; knot sealant; soaps.
The brushes, varnish, stains for covering up.

Promises: you can do it; it will work;
what's wear and tear to us? The busy till
nestles in paper bags, old labels, things
you can't put words to. Patching, making do;
a shop of second chances and amends.
Each time you're glad they haven't shut for good.

Swallow

For just one day a swallow fed her young
outside our rented window on high wires
stretched from the gable end above a street
where nothing happened. Two floors down
a door might open sometimes or a gate
click as a neighbour brought her shopping in
from morning shadows
                                        but up here
our air was hot with hunger
three feet from the glass, and rattling
in four loud throats. Their screams
swivelled to call in food, their noise
scraping the slates in desperate fear
of no-next-time, their brick-red faces
scarved in inky gloss. Born refugees,
they squirmed, already robed for flight,
no choice but travelling the treacherous air,
no safe frontiers to head for.

Next day they were gone, leaving
only an empty question on the wire.

Afendrika

Three churches, abandoned
to goat bells, francolins,
the hidden *hiss-huur* of the sea;

burnished with crown daisy, tarnished
with vetches, drifts of white scabious
whispering lines from their creed,

a gecko dazed on the stones, flat
and shadowless, one swallow
in, out, gone to the whistling sky

through the blue of a broken arch.
Written out of time, untenanted,
windowless and windswept, but

rooted deep in a blackened chancel
three honey-dark tapers, still smoking.

Stars

stare in through broken slates
and fallen ribs of rafters;
notes in a cobweb net.

No one left here to name them
out of need, or for a story
to bring them down to earth.

Not that they know of names or myth
imposed, dragged into our orbit
of love and lovers and desire

or even time in neat division.
Sirius, Andromeda, Orion;
lonely Aldebaran.

Any Other City

Vanishing point. You don't listen
for the cover of your own language,
but take a side-street from familiar accents.

Cold mornings taste of bells. The local saints
won't bless you, struggling with the words
for *please* or *help me.*

Shadows shrug your passing, dropping ash
next to the ash-tray, rustling
the morning anagram of news.

It could be worse. You could be
where you are known, where coffee
comes in creaking polystyrene,

where you can't smell the earth close up
under the streets, the orange blossom
in the plaza, and the south wind.

Not to be Loose Shunted

A hot wind bowls apologies
down Platform 1. A goods train clanks.
Aggregates heading south, each truck
stencilled with stern authority:
NOT TO BE LOOSE SHUNTED

caused by a defective

and they trundle, patient, bored,
deprived of every runaway thrill:

running approximately twenty minutes late

clank. Past the city's triumphs,
an angled greeting in four languages,
knee-high in weeds, and shedding flakes of paint
like dandruff. Clank. Clank.

for the inconvenience caused

Present Tense

You wake in the last room you slept in,
not this. Your clothes are tomorrow's,
chosen for who you'll meet, discreet,
laid out when you crept in late,
yesterday's time dropped behind the date line.
The sun sneaks in at a different angle
past the wrong curtains; you're certain
there must be a chair, a suitcase. No books.

Whatever the language is, it has no word
for this imbalance or for air
held inside the keyhole. If you offer its verbs a coffee
they will decline, turning away, distaste
pinching their lips. The mirror lies, its glass
a fog of past faces, none of them yours.

No Man's Land

A name might give you some co-ordinates:
vowels that hold a liquid tilt and splash,
the blending-in of travelled speech
before the temporary people left, before barbed wire
strung the guarded edges or made a wary perching place
for migrant birds and windswept plastic bags.

Your eyes make out how tall the trees have grown
out of abandoned roofs; how the towers,
their language twisted out of true, lean now
towards the sun, unsettling their foundations.
No one knows how many foxes have their holes
beneath the rubble of once-promised land.

A scrap of wild, bewildered holding-on,
anchored to where some roots are merging, here
and almost at your feet; nettles, fat hen.
Something in common greening up a sprawl of hedge,
the fattening grass, this watered blur of sky and earth
and light that listens without seeming to.

Bog Oak

One of those years. A skein of drying summers
quietly unpicking the knit of fen-stuff
eases them up, like it or not.

They look like yesterday, but meaner,
all muscle, setting hard as flint,
harder to shift. All the green disguise—

whispering leaves, shelter for owls,
a canopy to soften storms—
stripped back to tough menace:

what can we do with them, these old bullies,
out of their graves, threatening the fields?

From August Sander's Archive

He tells us there are no unexplained shadows
but when we stare into this long exposure—
their eyes and swallowed smiles,
their black and white straight lines—
something flickers near the edges.

It's not language (we've stabbed at translation,
title near-enough right) nor the angled jaunt
of hats, slim canes, a cigarette,
those polished boots avoiding Westerwald mud.
It's not the gleam of their razored austerity.

It's not light. We see everything
he wants us to see: *Jungbauern*, the habit
of scrubbed hands, three men brushed
into black-buttoned Sunday best
fixed on a path leading out of the frame.

They could be anywhere, these men, halfway
between leaving and arriving, looking
through the lens and into us, somewhere sunless;
no clue to how the compass lies, what the pull
beneath the tough attention of their stance.

This solid and clean-collared certainty,
confident their year is bringing home
only the victories of sex and silk,
prints them secure. No shadow of doubt
inside the darkroom's secret processes

and if we stand here, questioning what falls
across three farmers and a dance ahead,
1914, and too much to be answered,
the camera hasn't lied: it shows how far
the troubled shadows fall, how long they stain.

Absent

He learned fast: how to be
the empty circle, that ink of hollow space
among the cross-hatched eagerness of names
who queued to fill each team twice over;

how to slide to the edge, where long grass
ripples into undergrowth, the dapple
of light becoming camouflage, and sound
of his breathing blending with the trees.

Nothing to catch at, grab hold of
or wake with in the morning.
Up before the alarm went off, the door
closing in the draught, his phone unanswered.

Something minimal below the radar.
Later, AWOL, his eyes always
looking for exits, rat-runs, slips and corners.
Missing, at last, though this still unconfirmed.

P.O.W.

After the camp he returned,
folding himself,
bringing back nothing, except
this swivelling way of watching
everyone, everywhere.

She waited
while he stripped the chicken carcass,
every sliver, not a scrap wasted,
leaving the bones polished,
scoured of meat;
a gleam on the plate.

It was only over
with the last shred eliminated
and the silence reshaped around him.

Heroes of Our Islands

Dust jacket: faded (sun)
and water stained; torn,
front and back, repairs
(amateur); cracked spine
and wear to corners.
Cover (linen) worn.
Dog-eared, furring on all sides.
Maps partly crayonned in
and marginalia (juvenile).
Some illus., black and white; defaced.

Inscribed: *To dearest John,*
to speed you in their footsteps,
love
from Auntie Joan,
and kisses, Christmas 1959.

Was

She says nothing's what it was—this milk's
whitewash. And as for bread—jabbing
the toasting fork's warped prongs into its flab—

what can you say? The space between falls
across checked tablecloth, the coalman's bill.
An apple log turns ashes in the grate.

His photo mouths *Don't get her started!*
but the theme has shrugged off every ornament.
It's always been too late. She knows the script

by heart, how it's filled the silence since.
Her eyes search for scraps, for something more
but only the old bread made proper crumbs.

Souvenirs

They line up an impossible map—
Blackpool next to Minehead, Llandudno
alongside Brighton, the Isle of Wight
stuck in the middle with Edinburgh and Rhyl.
That was Doreen, the year after she married.

Skegness is a spill-jar, before
they put in central heating, made her
get rid of the grate. Scarborough
with its coat of arms slipping sideways
came from Jack and Lillian and the boys.

But Yarmouth is special. That was Bill
in 1939—his last gift—brought back
with bloaters: a saucer, and the town's crest
bright as his army buttons.

She still washes them once a month, dusts them
daily, settles them back, waiting—
for a letter, a call, a visit, someone
who can stir their tea and ask enough
to bring them home.

Background Effect

Always there, unspoken, in the photograph's
smudged greys: beyond smiling children caught
quiet for once, the dolls and tea-sets
and three-wheelers, and plastic beakers of squash
(remembered orange).

His Sunday work, following roast and gravy,
with the regular push and whirr rising
over garden fences, the roller squealing
for oily rest, old blades whispering
a popular ballad, the grass two-tone green.

It set everything off: the rolled-out stripes
in up-down order, straight as a ruler,
week in, week out, levelling
troubled patches, keeping the edges
sharp as a trouser crease.

You'd only notice if you looked, behind
the foreground of happy families,
into the back of the picture, the sun
slanting across and measuring seasons
against his unremarkable pattern.

Escape

Later, when the secretaries have switched off their machines
and the slow outward buses on the bridge bulge with faces
and we've given up giving the last rites to insoluble questions,
you talk about the coat.

How it hangs in your garage, ready.

How you wore it across the wire,
over fields, fearing guards and guns
and worse. How it covered your back,
and pulled the wool over their eyes.
How it saw you through,
translated you here.
How it's waiting
and
in the end
you'll go down into the earth together.

Losing Mr Winter

I lost Mr Winter last May, she says
as though he's somewhere back in the house,
the old van, or down the yard knee-deep
in the business, as he often was.
This fact lies in the leaves between us, October
whistling through its teeth wanting off,
the engine running and her grandson—
he can lift them two at a time—unloading
bags of compost for another season.
She was always the talker. He'd sit,
engine idling, one eye on her, counting,
letting his initial curl on the cheque.
Mister and missus to each other.
Was it—? Yes. The heart of the matter.

Common Ground

We peck for something suitable, weighing
the sayable while the black cars glide
untroubled into place. Small stuff,
drawing a line under
another of our parents' generation.
Too old for change, we let
children define us: travels, success,
their proud fertility. Outlines. Then
the scant few seconds scattering damp earth before
we shuffle, cough, offer the last excuse,
facing the long drive home.

We must meet up at other times, we say,
weaving good-byes, fingers crossed against
the M6, rush-hour tailbacks, evening rain.

Sea Interlude

A lucky morning and the sea
flat from shore to sky
and that line of clouds, tight
as a line of fine knitting.

Or possibly braided rope. One day
I won't be here to ask
Would you ever write that?
You, looking up, puzzled, saying *What?*

The Only View

It may come to this: one window
forcing its view of the world, framing
a red-brick gable end, the slanted line
of ridge-tiles flecked with scuffed cement,
two lanky buddleia waving from the slates,
blackened extractor belching burger gas,
its grill softened with soot, and dirty weather
fingering the glass under a sky
of sepia resentment. In the yard
you only know by ear, the lorries yawn
and cough after a frosty night and slam
their doors to grind off in the dark.
You count them out. At times a crow will squat
and shit and shift its weight and you'll be glad
it chose today. And even this
so beautiful you just can't bear to leave.

Leaving the World Service

It's still too dark to see the weather
or what the day is wearing. Minutes
are slowly hardening in their shells, setting
into hours ahead. The radio

talks us down, out of that far unknown
of dreams and other countries,
and the light comes on in the fridge,
next to the resentful kettle.

It's like a border crossing, where
the night shift waits the dawn relief of headlights,
owls in the valley silent. Or that pause
before the tide gulps at its new direction.

Out on the street a walker, hooded, faceless,
joins up deep shadows, swimming underwater
between the lamp posts; at the last pool of light
he vanishes until tomorrow.

One other car, sharing the early road;
an unnamed bus positioning its start
for the first sweepings of the working day.
Sludge of grit and salt, and that every-morning voice

shipping us out now, measuring the gales,
visibility, strengths, the inshore waters,
anchors for the unknown day
here: rough ground once more called *Home*.

Home

In tired lines at airport security,
past screens of unsmiling faces,
the probe of every imagined secret;

in sleepless hotel rooms, deodorised
to mask the lists of other bodies, where
the small mirror shrinks you;

in strip-lit waiting rooms, avoiding
what lies in corners, under chair legs, when
you are only statistical data;

in whispered white light, the fuzz
of far-off features, the curtains
nearly closing, nearly closed

your hand will feel for it, the grain
snug as a door frame,
the place that always welcomed you back.

Past

This parcel bulging in brown paper,
creased with old addresses, scraps of stamps,
the thumping clash of sorting offices;
packed with our own bread and language,
some embroidered samplers of names and dates,
a creation myth, the significantly lost battle.

Who wrapped its yellowing layers
in oily tissue, chose the forgotten books,
those wedding photographs we no longer recognise
and tucked the ends in, folding them tight
against curious eyes, the steel of questions?

Look at the string—knots we've lost the words for,
that tangle we struggle with, hardly
holding it together. Must I sign here?

The Rescue Dig

Forty years on you share the photographs:
evidence in black and white, a background
of measured trenches, string, and—how it comes back!—
that wobbly plank up the spoil heap,
the wrist-ache of Roman cobbles,
a post-hole's stain surrendering its soft dark.

Builders breathe down our necks. We are unearthing
older floor-plans, feeling our way back,
(not knowing how deep) through layers
built up as oh-so-casual time forgets its place,
undoes mosaics of deities, breaks up
the walls and proudly plastered certainties of home.

Each day brings us closer, crouched into the clay,
lifting each small loss into our summer:
their coins corrupted green, a brooch crushed
out of its latest fashion, glowing chips
of glossed flame-scarlet Samian. Behind the lens
you catch me, head down, worrying at a stone.

The builder's clock is ticking. He's laid roads
to roll the cul-de-sacs of semi-s out.
Another week he'll have us filled in, laughing
at how our scratching flattens out so fast.
Elsewhere, Paris still counts its wounds, while tanks
crush granite paving on the streets in Prague.

Details detain us: pits of oyster shells,
grooves worn in native rock by chariot wheels,
a Ford Anglia's angular back window,
poles, the tea-break caravan. My hair.
And who this other man might be, his face,
which must have been important to us, once.

Jack

Every family has one somewhere on the tree,
slipping out late with a cardboard suitcase,
enough to pay his passage. Or slamming out,
cracking the plaster, waking neighbours
who keep silence, knowing their own.
Or one-day-doesn't-come-in, and his girl
eyeing the calendar. Not great writers
the raw-skinned terraced lads. They know enough
not to look back: at the one photograph,
a musty wardrobe, the narrow bed.
Never buying a stamp for a postcard—
Statue of Liberty, or the Chicago skyline—
they leave all points of the compass possible.
Good with horses is how they're remembered,
handy with a hammer. Their names come up
at Christmas, or as birthdays mount,
or in dreams where they never age.
The elsewhere of them is the one constant
among deaths and births; with no date to mourn
they will swagger back one day, bigger than life,
a knock on the door to complete the circle.

Obsolete

When we married we thought they'd last for ever—
those Casa Pupo bowls, bone-handled knives, the glasses
and clock from Selfridges, and hand-painted tea set—
as well as all the families who gave us
candy-striped sheets, toasters, an ironing board,
the *Readers Digest Book of Household Repairs*

and a hammer. But now everything needs repairs—
frayed, chipped, burned out, or crazed—but who ever
these days, in this day and age. . . ? *Throw it all overboard*
says Electric Dreadlocks, too young for glasses,
it ain't worth the hassle, man—leaving us
without the habit of a trusted toaster, set

for breakfast. Five bowls from a set
of chunky Swedish (all the rage, once) smashed. Repairs
become a battleground: *do we? don't we?* What, to us,
was everlasting ends up on council tips; never ever
expected. Despite the crystal balls and similar mad glasses
unclouding the future, beyond the ouija board

and camp astrologers, Tarot in the Retiro (where the board,
gaudy as Carmen, promised sex and death), and the set
of loaded dice, nothing told the truth: that glasses
stain with lees, that mirrors break, that repairs
won't dodge the seven unlucky years, can't last for ever;
that time is not only catching up with us

but has overtaken, thundering confidently ahead—and us
breaking down on the hard shoulder, clapped out, and
                                        nothing on board
but a second-hand road map. If I didn't love you, now and for ever,
I'd walk out into the next tonnage of wheels, a personal sunset,

knowing the the NHS can't cope with such repairs
as we'll need soon: hips, knees, and eyes (our glasses

no longer enough.) But still, let's fill our glasses,
whether chipped or not, with decent wine, the Marsannay, just us,
and drink to night and sun and the sea, all that repairs
the obsolete wreck of hope and, setting up the board,
fumble another evening of chess—your set
from schooldays, your name and form inked deep, as if for ever.

Tomorrow we'll try a new place for repairs, but tonight the board
is spread with matchless bowls and glasses—relics of us.
Will we see a cloudless sunset? This sun can't last for ever.

Shibboleth

Only a hairline. Nothing, they said.
It doesn't matter.
There's nothing to say.

Perhaps it's nothing. Only a small crack
no deeper than surface.
Nothing to talk about.

Does it matter? Smooth it over.
Nothing will show.
Don't look at it now.

We can ignore it, can't we.
Can't we ignore it?
In some lights it's invisible.

It's barely visible.
And if it's no deeper . . .
Why can't we talk about something else?

Do we have to look at it?
It looks the same, doesn't it?
Doesn't it look the same?

I can't see why it matters.
Is it anything?
What is there to say?

It's just one of those things.
No one seems to know
how long this has been going on.

How long *has* this been going on?

Mostly

This is how it was: a dance perhaps, or
sometimes in the cinema's plush dark
lit by a match or cigarette. A walk
after the last bus was long gone: you know
those story lines, the comfort of fixed form
that frothed to wedding white (a virgin lie),
then ran its course. The black and white of it
framed on the sideboard, and the children came
neatly, at intervals; the template's fit
never quite right, but almost, till the time
a face, a look—a cup smashed on the floor,
doors slammed, unsilenced, all the house undone
by that new making, every smile and kiss.
Oh love, when were there ever rules for this?

Inheriting

We look at them now. More closely
even than the photographer's trained eye
deep inside the dark, we search for this:

some feature of connection—chin, or nose,
or brow. Like scene-of-crime police
we look at them. Now, more closely

floodlit in the glare of hindsight,
stripping their masks, secrets no longer
deep inside the dark, we search for this

to tell the children: here, with watch-chain or
lorgnette, is family. A knowing century on,
we look at them. Now. More closely

resemble them, wanting and not wanting
to reveal what is ingrained, which traits run
deep. Inside the dark we search for this

and ask, as others will, reading our photographs,
what failings we hold tightly
deep inside the dark. We search for this,
we look—and at them now, more closely.

After Chekhov

So cool and impractical in their washed linen,
the family are picking over finer points and arguing
directions and how the future glows or fades
                              behind the orchard,
and while the rugs are endlessly rearranged over grass
                              humming with summer,
you refill the samovar. The jug (from the kitchen,
and carried by the limping boy who is frightened of butterflies)
is cooler than your hands, and between the shadows knitted
by birch trees and a sulk of yellow scrub and the foreground
where all the action is, you refill the samovar.
A large family, expanding and contracting
as trains come and go, fuelled by disagreements,
and it's a full-time job setting tables, clearing half-eaten fruit,
sweeping crumbs, swatting flies, refilling the samovar.
They take for granted how effortless their summer is
in all the intensity of small talk and precedence—
that every glass is polished, the silver
                              (which they have yet to sell)
is still untarnished, that each day will float into a dusk
peopled with moths and temper and the latest arrivals,
including a school-master and, always, the doctor.
They won't notice you, refilling the samovar,
                              handing the cups,
watching the boy from the kitchen; or how they never reach
their answers or destinations, while you
achieve unmistakable silence, the near-impossible.

'His poems have been aired on BBC radio'

—contributor's note, 2013

I bring them in: the sheets,
line-fresh and flecked with apple blossom,
creased to a map of the wind; handkerchiefs—
white, tissue-thin—clutching the air's green scent
(a grassy nose, hard gooseberries,
an undertow of nettles); and the shirts
crackle-hard, defiantly dry,
to argue with the iron.

My mother made the fire work twice over,
loading her kitchen line each night, trapping
the coal's last heat in pillowslips before
next morning's mirror-test for damp, its faint
frail breath misting the glass. Between us
we know all there is to know about airing.

Are we nearly there yet?

The grown-ups smile, not wanting to answer,
contented with passing fields, a farm,
the slow silting of a river. Cloud shadows
race the car, winning at every stand of trees.

The backs of their heads share the joke.
They hand barley-sugar distractions, point
a church or cow or traffic sign; ask
only the *I-Spy* score.

Time itches to be whiled away
between here and there, quietly;
making the best of it, before
the stacked-up excitement, the planned and packed for
name on the calendar, the explosion

of sea and sunlight. Somewhere,
not marked on any map, lies an old boundary
the grown-ups crossed, innocent as swallows:
that line of learning, where
it's enough to be here, lengthening the moment.
They will be there, soon enough.

The Sunday Night Piano

Rolling in on the late train, halfway
between the weekend's open autumn fields
and Monday's ring-fenced desk, hearing
tired wheels rub the shine off the concourse,
dodging a sober pigeon checking crumbs,
the final Eurostar emptied, *lattes* gone stale,
you catch a first tangle of notes.

A cleaner halts, balanced
on the handle of a long day's mopping-up,
and listens. Blue iron arches
hold back the darkness, poised
over the phrasing. Is it Schubert?

He's left a *Lidl* bag slumped by his feet,
this man, last of the many players of the day,
bringing to life the loneliness
laid in the keys, his lover's touch
knowing by heart what's hidden. One by one
the shops put out their lights. The cleaner stirs
and shuffles with his mop. The steps
turning away to join the Northern Line
have never seemed so hard.

As it usually does

the wind gets up about this time
sneaky with just enough tug
flicking a page or loose hair
or somebody else's sweet wrapper
tipping over shingle and stone
and half-hearted patches of sand
children claim for storybook seaside
sandcastle business
the moat always leaking and the youngest
tottering with excitement egged on
by *careful!* and *watch it!*
the tide going out or coming in
appearing to do neither

and the question's there like a cloud
miles out to sea and small
only a scrap in the sky but it'll grow
when we have to give something sorry
to its goosebumped nagging
won't take no
insists until it's covering the whole sky
and *where did that come from?*
newspapers flapping like flags
picnics shredded, even the gulls
pitched off the rooftops and now
the weather's really coming rough
dragging the horizon.

The Wirral Family

I worry about them, growing feral
in the vague distance, beyond motorways
piled on beds of nameless rubble.
They never arrive, despite their babble
of promises, those Babel-excuses,
the rumble of their late-night phone-calls.

They live, they say, among such roaring winters
the sun is alien. They cannot follow bloodlines,
and their children are paler each year
longing only for the same story, every night.

The Whole Story

There were two of us—that's right, isn't it?—
knowing nothing beyond days slipping down
honeyed and sun-touched, and enough words
to cover the whole creation.

Is this what you want? There were birds
dangling their notes from easy branches,
a sprawl of flowers, grasses in fountains
of shimmer and light; a whole world.

You want it again? Colours
you've never dreamed of, silky with music,
the magic of forever in the air—and yet
that shape of something, missing.

What more can I say? I stretched out—
yes, this hand: look, the same movement,
everyday the same. Perhaps that was it,
but never knowing enough to make an answer.

You think you know it all, the first cloud,
the wind restless and smelling of rain,
like the invention of autumn. We were two
—and you? What would you have done?

Lot's Wife

Another of God's jokes, we said. A pillar
of salt, a nameless faceless fact.
Jinxed for her one last backward glance
to where home burned.

One of RE's more memorable plots. If this
were Chemistry there'd be the formula;
or Geography, erosion (rain and wind),
perhaps what farming and the economy gained.

She got on God's wrong side: simple enough
and easy (like the apple) for exams.
We'd spill it like dry beans, and pass.
Move on. Nothing to linger with, unless

the business by the daughters (rattled through
just at the end-of-lesson bell). We'd learned
enough to giggle, look away and out
and never think of ever looking back.

The Russian Doll

She'd split in half, a perfect crack along
her painted world's equator—north and south,
somewhere below the heart. This mass of secrets
makes her visible: her so-much-likeness
layered in generation, held with pride.

Never the right time. The nest, fevered
with family, itches within her, closed
against daylight, fearing some quake
could strip their trademark smiles back to the grain
or peel away their apron uniforms.

She feels them gasp for air; sits tight, keeps whole
the seethe of hidden questions, stops her ears
against their hum. For just as long
as they can stick together they'll outface
the change of necessary splintering.

Responsibilities

The children's eyes, smudged black with lack of sleep,
glare disapproval. *What time d'you think. . . ?*
they splutter when we stay out late
breaking the rules again. *And in those clothes!*
They shiver, gazing up in brave reproach.
We told you: take a coat. Once
they set a curfew, gated us until
we cleaned our room and lied that we'd behave.
Some chance ! They confide in friends
over school lunches: where did they go wrong?
and will we ever learn? They whisper how
they have to check our bags, can't trust us
with the car. What if we're taken into care?
That they're too young for this.

At Swim

In the deep ocean his stroke's
a stride, kicking
from island to island,
churning the tropical salt
to muscular waves, his trunk
a rearing snorkel releasing
shoals of bubbles.

Riding his neck, the mahout
tickles his ears like a fish, leading
this lack of gravity through
his new element,
all the weight of the world
washed away.

The Best of It

Remember that beach-ball?
The child wailing family watching
no one knowing what to do for the best
and the ball quite a small ball making its own way out
red and yellow over a flat sea no breeze
the invisible tide pulling faster faster
beyond the fishermen's buoys
over the drowned lobster pots
past a couple of gulls who took no notice,
straight out. On the beach they start the *how?*
and *why?* and who gets the blame
or the ice cream to smooth it over
and forget everything except each other while the ball—
even smaller now, even further out—
rides to the horizon like a hero
with his mind on the prize, high-minded
and sure of himself at last and free
from all that squabble and trouble.
No going back now; on course
for the grail or whatever lies
where the sea and sky stop.
No one to cheer him on and—look!
Out of sight already.

ACKNOWLEDGEMENTS

Some of these poems, or earlier versions, were published in
*Anon, Antiphon, Assent, Brittle Star, Envoi, 14, Iota, Literary
Review, Magma, New Walk, Other Poetry, Pennine Platform,
Poetry News, Poetry Nottingham International, Prole, Smiths Knoll,
South, South Bank Poetry, Snakeskin, Staple, The Frogmore Papers,
The Interpreter's House, The North, The Rialto, Under the Radar.*

'All the time in the world' was included in the first *James
Kirkup Memorial Anthology*, 2010 (Red Squirrel Press).

'From August Sander's Archive' first appeared in the *Ware
Competition Anthology*, 2010.

'Background effect' and 'Jack' were featured on the Poetry
Society website (Stanza Poetry Competitions 2010 & 2012).

'Inheriting' was included in *Soundswrite 2011 Anthology*.